Microsoft OneNote 2016 Keyboard Shortcuts

For Macintosh

By

U. C-Abel Books.

All Rights Reserved

First Edition: 2016

Copyright @ U. C-Abel Books. ISBN-13: 978-1537117058

ISBN-13: 978-1537117058
ISBN-10: 153711705X

Published by U. C-Abel Books.

Table of Contents

Acknowledgement.

U. C-Abel Books will not take all credits for Microsoft OneNote 2016 keyboard shortcuts listed in this book, but shares it with Microsoft Corporation because some of the shortcuts came from them and are "used with permission from Microsoft".

Dedication

This compilation is dedicated to Mac computer users and lovers of keyboard shortcuts all over the world.

Introduction.

We enjoy using shortcuts because they set us on a high plane that astonishes people around us when we work with them. As wonderful shortcuts users, the worst eyesore we witness in computer operation is to see somebody sluggishly struggling to execute a task through mouse usage when in actual sense shortcuts will help to save that person time. Most people have asked us to help them with a list of keyboard shortcuts that can make them work as smartly as we do and that drove us into research to broaden our knowledge and truly help them as they demanded, that is the reason for the existence of this book. It is a great tool for lovers of shortcuts, and those who want to join the group.

Most times the things we love don't come by easily. It is our love for keyboard shortcuts that made us to bear long sleepless nights like owls just to make sure we get the best out of it, and it is the best we got that we are sharing with you in this book. You cannot be the same at computing after reading this book. The time you entrusted to our care is an expensive possession and we promise not to mess it up.

Thank you.

What to Know Before You Begin.

General Notes.

1. For effective use of keyboard shortcuts listed in this book, JAWS users must turn off Virtual Ribbon Menu feature.
2. Most of the keyboard shortcuts you will see in this book refer to the U.S. keyboard layout. Keys for other layouts might not correspond exactly to the keys on a U.S. keyboard. Keyboard shortcuts for laptop computers might also differ.
3. It is important to note that when using shortcuts to perform any command, you should make sure the target area is active, if not you may get a wrong result. Example, if you want to highlight all texts you must make sure the text field is active and if an object, make sure the object area is active. The active area is always known by the location where the cursor of your computer blinks.
4. On a Mac keyboard, the Command key is denoted with the ⌘symbol.
5. The settings in some versions of the Macintosh operating system and some utility applications might conflict with keyboard shortcuts and function key operations in Office.
6. If a function key doesn't work as you expect it to, press the Fn key in addition to the function key. If you don't want to press the Fn key every time, you can change your Apple system preferences.

7. The plus (+) sign that comes in the middle of keyboard shortcuts simply means the keys are meant to be combined or held down together not to be added as one of the shortcut keys. In a case where plus sign is needed; it will be duplicated (++).
8. Many keyboards assign special functions to function keys, by default. To use the function key for other purposes, you have to press Fn+the function key.
9. For keyboard shortcuts in which you press one key immediately followed by another key, the keys are separated by a comma (,).

10. It is also important to note that the keyboard shortcuts listed in this book are for Microsoft OneNote 2016 for Mac.

Other Areas to Take Note of.

Common Office For Mac Keyboard Shortcuts

The common office for mac keyboard shortcuts listed in this book are applicable to Excel 2016 for Mac, PowerPoint 2016 for Mac, Word for Mac 2016, Outlook 2016 for Mac, Word for Mac 2011, Excel for Mac 2011, Outlook for Mac 2011, and PowerPoint for Mac 2011.

Create a custom keyboard shortcut for Office 2016 for Mac.

The steps written on how to create a custom keyboard shortcuts for office 2016 for mac applies to all of its programs.

OneNote for Mac

Keyboard shortcuts listed in this section are for use in OneNote for Mac 2016.

Some Short Forms You Will Find in This Book and Their Full Meaning.

Here are short forms used in this Microsoft OneNote 2016 Keyboard Shortcuts For Macintosh book and their full meaning.

1.	Win	-	Windows logo key
2.	Tab	-	Tabulate Key
3.	Shft	-	Shift Key
4.	Prt sc	-	Print Screen
5.	Num Lock	-	Number Lock Key
6.	F	-	Function Key
7.	Esc	-	Escape Key
8.	Ctrl	-	Control Key
9.	Caps Lock	-	Caps Lock Key
10.	Alt	-	Alternate Key

CHAPTER 1.

About Office 2016 and Mac.

Introduction to Microsoft Office.

Microsoft Office is a computer software made up of apps, servers and services, developed and marketed by Microsoft Corporation.

Definition of Macintosh.

Macintosh is a popular model of computer manufactured and marketed by Apple Inc. that features a graphical user interface which uses windows, icons, and a mouse to make it relatively easy for newbies/novices to use the computer effectively.

Differences between (Macintosh) Macs and Personal Computers (Pcs). By www.diffen.com

A **PC** generally refers to a computer that runs on the Windows operating system. It is also defined as an IBM-compatible computer, thereby meaning that its architecture is based on the IBM microprocessor. A number of different operating systems are compatible with PCs; the most popular of which is Microsoft Windows. Some others are the UNIX variants, such as Linux, FreeBSD, and Solaris.

On the other hand **Macintosh**, commonly known as **Mac**, is a brand name which covers several lines of personal computers designed, developed, and marketed by Apple Inc. The Mac is the only computer in the world that can run all the major operating systems, including Mac OS X, Windows XP, and Vista. With software like Parallels Desktop or VMware Fusion they can be run; side by side.

Macs and PCs both have dedicated followers, and each type of computer has its own strengths and weaknesses.

Mac		PC
What is it?	Short form for "Macintosh" and refers to any computer produced by Apple, Inc.	Refers to any computer running IBM-Based (Windows, Linux, Solaris, FreeBSD) operating systems. stands for "Personal Computer"
Cost	Computers start at $499 for the Mac Mini desktop, $899 for the Macbook Air notebook, and	Compared to a Mac, Windows and Windows-associated hardware is

	$1099 for the iMac all-in-one. Other models are more expensive. For desktop or home use Macs are generally expensive than a PC.	cheaper, and you can build your own for even less money. Comparable computers running Windows can be found around 40% cheaper than a Mac.
Manufacturer	Apple Inc	Several companies: HP, Toshiba, Dell, Lenovo, Samsung, Acer, Gateway etc.
Development and Distribution	Macs are developed and distributed by Apple Inc.	PCs are manufactured and distributed by hundreds of manufacturers.
Company / developer	Apple, Inc.	Microsoft (Windows), Ubuntu (Linux), Sun (Solaris), etc.
Gaming	Not as many games are made natively for the Mac, although in recent years, many more applications are released for them. The App Store is a hub for users to	The library of games available for the PC is exhaustive, and hardware specifically tweaked for gaming

	download games from.	performance is much more readily available for Windows. The array of graphics cards and upgradability also favor Windows-based computers.
User	Home users and businesses (mainly in the creative department)	Home users and businesses
Available language(s)	Multilingual	Must purchase a different OS Version, but has multiple languages available.
OS family	Unix-like (BSD>Darwin>Mac)	Windows, Linux, Solaris, FreeBSD, etc.
Popular Applications	Photos, iMovie, GarageBand, Pages, Numbers, Keynote, Safari, Mail, Messages, FaceTime, Calendar, Contacts, App Store, iTunes, iBooks, Maps, Photo Booth, Time Machine	MS Office, Internet Explorer, Media Player, Media Center, Windows Defender, SkyDrive, VLC media player, Chrome browser

Latest Operating System	OS X Yosemite (version 10.10); OS X El Capitan (version 10.11) announced	Windows 8/8.1, Windows 10 announced
Compatibility	Can open almost all PC files and can coexist on local networks with PCs. Can open .doc, .exe (as a compressed bundle), .xls, and others. Software exists for other file types. Can also run Windows on a Mac for 100% compatibility.	Mac-based files (.DMG) cannot be opened on PCs natively, but you can install software that can read, and possibly write Mac-based files on a PC.
Supported architectures	Intel Microprocessors	Intel and AMD processors
Market Reach	Attracts graphic designers, video and music producers, tech journalists, app developers etc.	Wide reach to all stratas. Business users tend to use Windows hardware due to compatibility.
Virus Attacks	Since Macs are not as popular as PCs, there are fewer malware written to target Macs, although the threat of malicious software is growing, like from Java.	Being the popular desktop choice, most virus writers target Windows systems, however, Linux often has less malware.

Compatible Operating Systems	OS X, Windows (through virtual machine or Boot Camp), Linux	Windows, Linux
Performance	Since Apple have controlled the hardware & software bundles and model updates, so every Mac operates smoothly without worry on lagging, incompatibles, and have stable and expected performance	Different OEMs and even custom build PCs might not have the suitable drivers released for every components in each OS version, incompatibles, lagging may occur. Maybe cannot reach expected performance
Repairs	Any knowledgeable person can perform repairs and upgrades. Local computer-help stores can also be contacted for repairs. AppleCare can extend the warranty. Newer Macs are becoming less upgrade-friendly, though.	Any knowledgeable person can perform repairs and upgrades. Local computer-help stores can also be contacted for repairs. OEMs and component shops provides limited warranty.

Programs and apps	Same as gaming, limited choice due to user range.	Same as gaming, excess choice due to user range.
Piracy Prevention	Activation is not required, can reinstall as many times as needed.	Windows has a unique activation key for each package distribution, and lots of custom and OEM PC appears, so genuine checking become important. Linux, Solaris, FreeBSD is free and no need for those keys.
Customizability	No	Yes
Messaging	Messages (using iMessage, Google Talk, etc.)	Skype, Facebook, and Twitter
Voice commands	Yes	Yes
Maps	Yes	Yes
Internet browsing	Safari, Chrome, Firefox, plus many more.	Internet Explorer, Chrome, Firefox, Safari (no longer supported)
App store	App Store	Windows Store
Widgets	Yes	Yes

Working state	Current	Current
Interface	Mouse, keyboard, trackpad, other peripherals	Mouse, keyboard, trackpad, other peripherals
Has Registry	No	Yes
Overclockable	No	Yes, depends on CPU and Motherboard

Introduction to Office 2016 for Mac.

Office 2016 is an office suite developed and sold by Microsoft. The preview version of Microsoft Office for Mac was released on 5th March 2015, then the final version was released on 5th July 2015 by Microsoft Corporation.

Supported languages in Office 2016 for Mac

Office 2016 for Mac is currently available in the following languages:

- Arabic
- Brazilian Portuguese
- Chinese (Simplified)
- Chinese (Traditional)
- Czech
- Danish
- Dutch
- English

- Finnish
- French
- Hebrew
- German
- Italian
- Japanese
- Norwegian Bokmal
- Polish
- Russian
- Spanish
- Swedish
- Thai

The Difference between Office 365 and Office 2016.

Office 365 is a subscription service (this means you pay for it on monthly or yearly basis) provided by Microsoft Corporation that includes the most recent version of office, which currently is also called office 2016. Some of the office 365 plans like HOME, let you share your subscription with people around you.

Contrariwise, Office 2016 is marketed as a one-time purchase bundle, this simply means you pay a single upfront cost to receive Office programs/applications for your personal or Macintosh computer. No upgrade option.

The major difference is that Office 365 has an upgrade option while office 2016 doesn't, this means that after you have purchased Office 2016 bundle, you will have to purchase another in future if there is an upgrade (added feature) you desire.

CHAPTER 2.

Fundamental Knowledge of Keyboard Shortcuts.

Without the existence of keyboard, there wouldn't have been anything like keyboard shortcuts so in this chapter we will learn a little about the computer keyboard before moving to keyboard shortcuts.

1. Definition of Computer Keyboard.

This is an input device that is used to send data to computer memory.

Sketch of a Keyboard

1.1 Types of Keyboard.

i. Standard (Basic) Keyboard.

ii. Enhanced (Extended) Keyboard.

i. **Standard Keyboard:** This is a keyboard designed during the 1800s for mechanical typewriters with just 10 function keys (F keys) placed at the left side of it.

ii. **Enhanced Keyboard:** This is the current 101 to 102-key keyboard that is included in almost all the personal computers (PCs) of nowadays, which has 12 function keys at the top side of it.

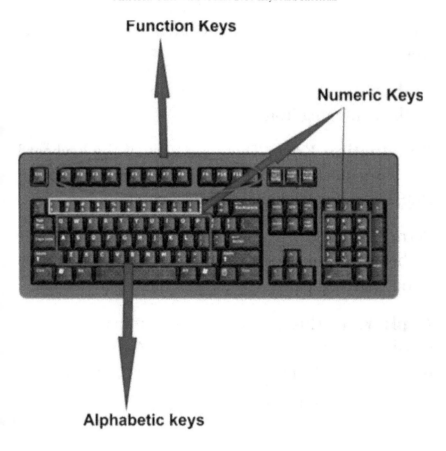

1.2 Segments of the keyboard

- Numeric keys
- Alphabetic keys
- Punctuation keys
- Windows Logo key.
- Function keys
- Special keys

Numeric Keys: Numeric keys are keys with numbers from **0 - 9**.

Alphabetic Keys: These are keys that have alphabets on them, ranging from **A** to **Z**.

Punctuation Keys: These are keys of the keyboard used for punctuation, examples include comma, full stop, colon, question marks, hyphen, etc.

Windows Logo Key: A key on Microsoft Computer keyboard with its logo displayed on it. Search for this *on your keyboard.

Apple Key: This also known as Command key is a modifier key that you can find on an Apple keyboard. It usually has the image of an apple or command logo on it. Search for this on your Apple keyboard

Function Keys: These are keys that have **F** on them which are usually combined with other keys. They are F1 - F12, and are also in the class called *Special Keys*.

Special Keys: These are keys that perform special functions. They include: Tab, Ctrl, Caps lock, Insert, Prt sc, alt gr, Shift, Home, Num lock, Esc and many others. Special keys differs according to the type of computer involved. In some keyboard layout, especially laptops, the keys that turn the speaker on/off, the one that increases/decreases volume, the key that turns the computer Wifi on/off are also special keys.

Other Special Keys Worthy of Note.

Enter Key: This is located at the right-hand corner of most keyboards. It is used to send messages to the computer to execute commands, in most cases it is used to mean "Ok" or "Go".

Escape Key (ESC): This is the first key on the upper left of most keyboards. It is used to cancel routines, close menus and select options such as **Save** according to circumstance.

Control Key (CTRL): It is located on the bottom row of the left and right hand side of the keyboard. They also work with the function keys to execute commands using Keyboard shortcuts (key combinations).

Alternate Key (ALT): It is located on the bottom row also of some keyboard, very close to the CTRL key on both side of the keyboard. It enables many editing functions to be accomplished by using some keystroke combinations on the keyboard.

Shift Key: This adds to the roles of function keys. In addition, it enables the use of alternative function of a particular button (key), especially, those with more than one function on a key. E.g. use of capital letters, symbols and numbers.

1.3. Selecting/Highlighting With Keyboard.

This is a highlighting method or style where data is selected using keyboard instead of a computer mouse.

To do this:

- Move your cursor to the text you want to highlight, make sure that area is active
- Hold down the shift key with one finger
- Then use another finger to move the arrow key that points to the direction you want to highlight.

1.4 The Operating Modes Of The Keyboard.

Just like mouse, keyboard has two operating modes. The two modes are Text Entering Mode and Command Mode.

a. **Text Entering Mode:** this mode gives the operator/user the opportunity to type text.
b. **Command Mode:** this is used to command the operating system/software/application to execute commands in certain ways.

2. Ways To Improve In Your Typing Skill.

1. Put Your Eyes Off The Keyboard.

This is the aspect of keyboard usage that many don't find funny because they always ask. "How can I put my eyes off the keyboard when I am running away from the occurrence of errors on my file?" My aim is to be fast, is this not going to slow me down?

Of course, there will be errors and at the same time your speed will slow down but the motive behind the introduction to this method is to make you faster than you are. Looking at your keyboard while you type can make you get a sore neck, it is better you learn to touch type because the more you type with your eyes fixed on the screen instead of the keyboard, the faster you become.

An alternative to keeping your eyes off your keyboard is to use the "*Das Keyboard Ultimate*".

2. Errors Challenge You

It is better to fail than not trying at all. Not trying at all is an attribute of the weak and lazybones. When you make mistakes, try again because errors are opportunities for improvement.

3. Good Posture (Position Yourself Well).

Do not adopt an awkward position while typing. You should get everything on your desk organized or arranged before sitting to type. Your posture while typing contributes to your speed and productivity.

4. Practice

Here is the conclusion of everything said above. You have to practice your shortcuts constantly. The practice alone is a way of improvement. "Practice brings improvement". Practice always.

2.1 Software That Will Help You Improve Your Typing Skill.

There are several Software programs for typing that both kids and adults can use for their typing skill. Here is a list of software that can help you improve in your typing: Mavis Beacon, Typing Instructor, Mucky Typing Adventure, Rapid Tying Tutor, Letter Chase Tying Tutor, Alice Touch Typing Tutor and many more. Personally, I recommend Mavis Beacon.

To learn typing with MAVIS BEACON, install Mavis Beacon software to your computer, start with keyboard lesson, then move to games. Games like **_Penguin Crossing, Creature Lab_** or **_Space Junk_** will help you become a professional in typing. Typing and keyboard shortcuts work hand-in-hand.

Sketch of a computer mouse

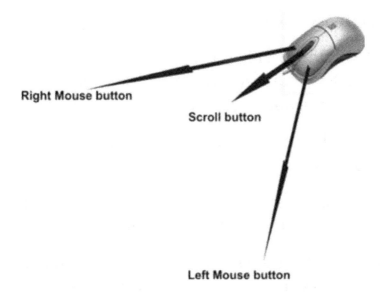

Right Mouse button

Scroll button

Left Mouse button

3. Mouse:

This is an oval-shaped portable input device with three buttons for scrolling, left clicking, and right clicking that enables work to be done effectively on a computer. The plural form of mouse is mice.

3.1 Types of Computer Mouse

- Mechanical Mouse
- Optical Mechanical Mouse (Optomechanical)
- Laser Mouse
- Optical Mouse
- BlueTrack Mouse

3.2 Forms of Clicking:

Left Clicking: This is the process of clicking the left side button of the mouse. It can also be called *clicking* without the addition of *left*.

Right Clicking: It is the process of clicking the right side button of a computer mouse.

Double Clicking: It is the process of clicking the left side button two times (twice) and immediately.

Double clicking is used to select a word while thrice clicking is used to select a sentence or paragraph.

Scroll Button: It is the little key attached to the mouse that looks like a tiny wheel. It takes you up and down a page when moved.

3.3 Mouse Pad: This is a small soft mat that is placed under the mouse to make it have a free movement.

3.4 Laptop Mouse Touchpad

This unlike the mouse we explained above is not external, rather it is inbuilt (comes with a laptop computer). With the presence of a laptop mouse touchpad, an external mouse is not needed to use a laptop, except in a case where it is malfunctioning or the operator prefers to use external one for some reasons.

The laptop mouse touchpad is usually positioned at the end of the keyboard section of a laptop computer. It is rectangular in shape with two buttons positioned below it. The two buttons/keys are used for left and right clicking just like the external mouse. Some laptops come with four mouse keys. Two placed above the mouse for left and right clicking and two other keys placed below it for the same function.

4. Definition Of Keyboard Shortcuts.

Keyboard shortcuts are defined as a series of keys, sometimes with combination that execute tasks that typically involve the use of mouse or other input devices.

5. Why You Should Use Shortcuts.

1. One may not be able to use a computer mouse easily because of disability or pain.

2. One may not be able to see the mouse pointer as a result of vision impairment, in such case what will the person do? The answer is SHORTCUT.

3. Research has made it known that Extensive mouse usage is related to Repetitive Syndrome Injury (RSI) greatly than the use of keyboard.

4. Keyboard shortcuts speed up computer users, making learning them a worthwhile effort.

5. When performing a job that requires precision, it is wise that you use the keyboard instead of mouse, for instance, if you are dealing with Text Editing, it is better you handle it using keyboard shortcuts than spending more time with your computer mouse alone.

6. Studies calculate that using keyboard shortcuts allows working 10 times faster than working with the mouse. The time you spend looking for the mouse and then getting the cursor to the position you want is lost! Reducing your work duration by 10 times brings you greater results.

5.1 Ways To Become A Lover Of Shortcuts.

1. Always have the urge to learn new shortcut keys associated with the programs you use.
2. Be happy whenever you learn a new shortcut.

3. Try as much as you can to apply the new shortcuts you learnt.

4. Always bear it in mind that learning new shortcuts is worth it.

5. Always remember that the use of keyboard shortcuts keeps people healthy while performing computer activities.

5.2 How To Learn New Shortcut Keys

1. Do a research for them: quick reference (a cheat sheet comprehensively compiled like ours) can go a long way to help you improve.

2. Buy applications that show you keyboard shortcuts every time you execute an action with mouse.

3. Disconnect your mouse if you must learn this fast.

4. Read user manuals and help topics (Whether offline or online).

5.3 Your Reward For Knowing Shortcut Keys.

1. You will get faster unimaginably.

2. Your level of efficiency will increase.

3. You will find it easy to use.

4. Opportunities are high that you will become an expert in what you do.

5. You won't have to go for **Office button**, click **New,** click **Blank and Recent** and click **Create** just to insert a fresh/blank page. **Ctrl +N** takes care of that in a second.

A Funny Note: Keyboarding and Mousing are in a marital union with Keyboarding being the head, so it will be unfair for anybody to put asunder between them.

5.4 Why We Emphasize On The Use of Shortcuts.

You may never ditch your mouse completely unless you are ready to make your brain a box of keyboard shortcuts which will really be frustrating, just imagine yourself learning all shortcuts that go with the programs you use and their various versions. You shouldn't learn keyboard shortcuts that way.

Why we are emphasizing on the use of shortcuts is because mouse usage is becoming unusually common and unhealthy, too. So we just want to make sure both are combined so you can get fast, productive and healthy in your computer activities. All you need to know is just the most important ones associated with the programs you use.

CHAPTER 3.

How to Download, Install, Launch, and Uninstall Office 2016 for Mac.

Download and Install Office 2016 for Mac

1. Go to your **My Account** page at Office.com and sign in with your Microsoft account.
2. On the **My Account** page, under the name of your subscription, select **Install**.

3. On the next page, under **Install information**, select **Install** to begin downloading the installation package.

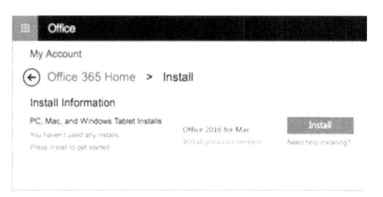

4. Once the download has completed, open Finder, go to **Downloads**, and double-click **Microsoft_Office_2016_Installer.pkg** (the name might vary slightly).

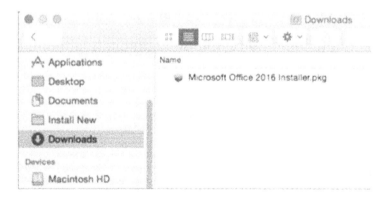

Tip: If you see an error that the Microsoft_Office_2016_Installer.pkg can't be opened because it is from an unidentified developer, wait 10 seconds and then try double-clicking the installer package again. If you are stuck at the **Verifying....**

progress bar, close or cancel the progress bar and try again.

5. On the first installation screen, select **Continue** to begin the installation process.

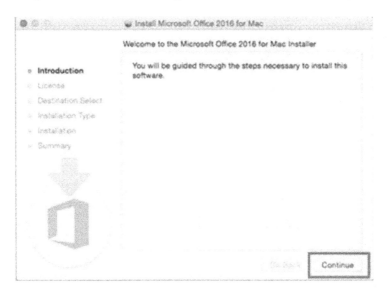

6. Review the software license agreement, and then click **Continue**.
7. Select **Agree** to agree to the terms of the software license agreement.
8. Review the disk space requirements, and then click **Install**.
9. Enter your Mac login password, if prompted, and then click **Install Software**. (This is the password that you use to log in to your Mac.)

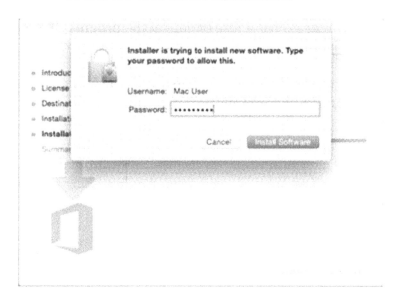

10. The software begins to install. Click **Close** when the installation is finished.

Launch an Office for Mac app and start the activation process.

1. Click the **Launchpad** icon in the Dock to display all of your apps.

2. Click the **Microsoft Word** icon in the Launchpad.

3. The **What's New** window opens automatically when you launch Word. Click **Get Started** to start activating.

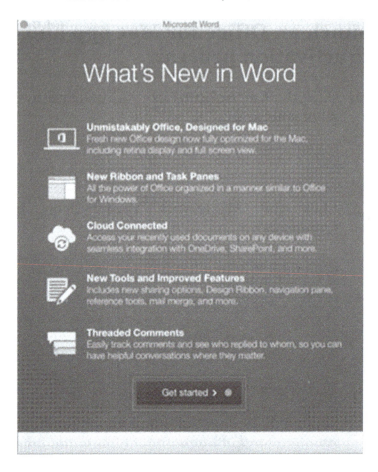

Installation notes

Can I install Office 2016 for Mac and Office for Mac 2011 on the same computer?

Yes, you can install and use Office 2016 for Mac and Office for Mac 2011 at the same time just like Office 2016 and Office 2013 for Windows. However, we recommend that you uninstall Office for Mac 2011 before you install the new version just to prevent any confusion.

How do I pin the Office app icons to the dock?

1. Go to **Finder** > **Applications** and open the Office app you want.
2. In the Dock, Control+click or right-click the app icon and choose **Options** > **Keep in Dock**.

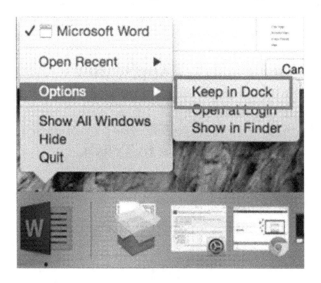

Uninstall Office 2016 for Mac.

Applies To: Excel 2016 for Mac, Outlook 2016 for Mac, PowerPoint 2016 for Mac, Word 2016 for Mac, and OneNote 2016 for Mac.

To uninstall Office 2016 for Mac, move the applications and user preference files to the Trash. Once you've removed everything, empty the Trash and restart your Mac to complete the process.

You must be signed in as an administrator or provide an administrator name and password to complete these steps.

Remove Office 2016 for Mac Applications.

1. Open Finder and click **Applications**.
2. Command ⌘+click to select all of the Office 2016 for Mac applications.
3. Ctrl+click or right-click the applications you selected and click **Move to Trash**.

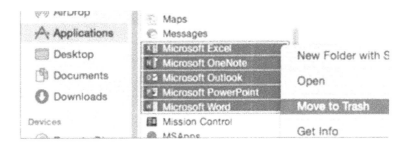

Remove Files from Your User Library Folder.

To remove files from your user **Library** folder, you'll need to first set the Finder View options.

1. In Finder, press ⌘+**Shift+h**.
2. On the Finder menu, click **View** > **as List**, and then click **View** > **Show View Options**.

3. In the **View Options** dialog box, select **Show Library Folder**.

4. Switch back to Column view (⌘+3) and click **<YourUserName>Library** > **Containers** and ctrl+click or right-click each of these folders if present, and then click **Move to Trash**.
   o **com.microsoft.errorreporting**
   o **com.microsoft.Excel**
   o **com.microsoft.netlib.shipassertproc ess**
   o **com.microsoft.Office365ServiceV2**
   o **com.microsoft.Outlook**
   o **com.microsoft.Powerpoint**
   o **com.microsoft.RMS-XPCService**
   o **com.microsoft.Word**
   o **com.microsoft.onenote.mac**

5. **Warning:** Outlook data will be removed when you move the three folders listed in this step to **Trash**. You should back up these folders before you delete them.

   Switch back to Column view (⌘+3) and click **<YourUserName>Library** > **Group**

Containers and ctrl+click or right-click each of these folders if present, and then click **Move to Trash**.

- ○ **UBF8T346G9.ms**
- ○ **UBF8T346G9.Office**
- ○ **UBF8T346G9.OfficeOsfWebHost**

CHAPTER 4.

15 (Fifteen) Special Keyboard Shortcuts.

The fifteen special keyboard shortcuts are fifteen (15) shortcuts every computer user should know.

The following is a list of keyboard shortcuts every computer user should know.

1. **Ctrl + A:** Control plus A, highlights or selects everything you have in the environment where you are working.

   *If you are like **"Wow, the content of this document is large and there is no time to select all of it, besides, it's going to mount pressure on my computer?"** Using the mouse for this is an outdated method of handling a task like selecting all, Ctrl+A will take care of that in a second.*

2. **Ctrl + C:** Control plus C copies any highlighted or selected element within the work environment.

   Saves the time and stress which would have been used to right click and click again just to copy. Use ctrl+c.

3. **Ctrl + N:** Control plus N opens a new window. *Instead of clicking* **File, New, blank/ template** *and another* **click,** *just press* ***Ctrl + N*** *and a fresh window will appear* *instantly.*

4. **Ctrl + O:** Control plus O opens a new program. *Use ctrl +O when you want to locate / open a file or program.*

5. **Ctrl + P:** Control plus P prints the active document. *Always use this to locate the printer dialog box, and thereafter print.*

6. **Ctrl + S:** Control plus S saves a new document or file and changes made by the user. *Please stop! Don't use the mouse. Just press Ctrl+S and everything will be saved.*

7. **Ctrl +V:** Control plus V pastes copied elements into the active area of the program in use. *Using ctrl+V in a case like this Saves the time and stress of right clicking and clicking again just to paste.*

8. **Ctrl + W:** Control plus W is used to close the page you are working on when you want to leave the work environment.

"There is a way Debby does this without using the mouse. Oh my God, why didn't I learn it then?" Don't worry, I have the answer. Debby presses Ctrl+W to close active windows.

9. **Ctrl + X:** Control plus X cuts elements (making the elements to disappear from their original place). The difference between cutting and deleting elements is that in Cutting, what was cut doesn't get lost permanently but prepares itself so that it can be pasted on another location selected by the user.

*Use ctrl+x when you think **"this shouldn't be here and I can't stand the stress of retyping or redesigning it in the rightful place it belongs".***

10. **Ctrl + Y:** Control plus Y redoes an undone action.

Ctrl+Z brought back what you didn't need? Press Ctrl+ Y to remove it again.

11. **Ctrl + Z:** Control plus Z undoes actions.
Can't find what you typed now or a picture you inserted, it suddenly disappeared or you mistakenly removed it? Press Ctrl+Z to bring it back.

12. **Alt + F4:** Alternative plus F4 closes active windows or items.

*You don't need to move the mouse in order to close an active window, just press **Alt** + **F4** if you are done or don't want somebody who is coming to see what you are doing.*

13. **Ctrl + F6:** Control plus F6 Navigates between open windows, making it possible for a user to see what is happening in windows that are active.

    Are you working in Microsoft Word and want to find out if the other active window where your browser is loading a page is still progressing? Use Ctrl + F6.

14. **F1:** This displays the help window.

    *Is your computer malfunctioning? Use **F1** to find help when you don't know what next to do.*

15. **F12:** This enables user to make changes to an already saved document.

    F12 is the shortcut to use when you want to change the format in which you saved your existing document, password it, change its name, change the file location or destination, or make other changes to it. It will save your time.

CHAPTER 5.

Common Office for Mac Keyboard Shortcuts.

Here are common shortcuts you can use when working with your Mac computer.

Working With Files, Applications, And Tools

TASK	SHORTCUT
Create a new file or Outlook item	Command + N
Create a new file from a template or theme	SHIFT + Command + P
Expand or minimize the ribbon	Command + OPTION + R
Save	Command + S
Print	Command + P
Open a file	Command + O
Close a file	Command + W
Quit the current application	Command + Q
Hide the current application	Command + H
Hide other applications	OPTION + Command + H
Minimize the window	Command + M

Editing And Formatting

TASK	SHORTCUT
Undo the last change	Command + Z
Redo or repeat the last action	Command + Y
Cut the selection (and copy to clipboard)	Command + X
Copy the selection to the clipboard	Command + C
Copy the formatting from the selection	Command + SHIFT + C
Copy the selection to Scrapbook	CONTROL + OPTION + C
Paste	Command + V
Paste Special	Command + CONTROL + V
Paste the formatting to the selection	Command + SHIFT + V
Select All	Command + A
Find	Command + F
Insert hyperlink	Command + K

Dialog Boxes

TASK	SHORTCUT
Move to the next text box in a dialog box	TAB
Move to the previous box, option, control, or command in a dialog box	SHIFT + TAB
Exit a dialog box or cancel an action	ESC

Create A Custom Keyboard Shortcut For Office 2016 For Mac.

To create custom keyboard shortcuts in Office for Mac, use the built-in capability in Mac OS X.

1. From the **Apple** menu, click **System Preferences** > **Keyboard** > **Shortcuts** > **App Shortcuts**.
2. Click the + sign to add a keyboard shortcut.

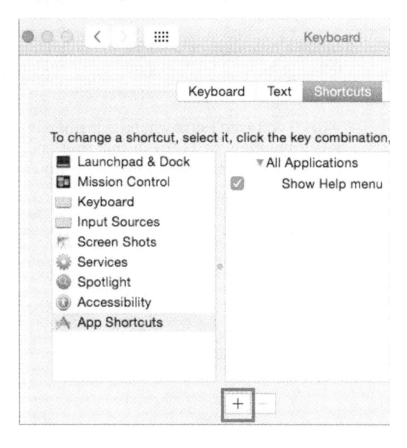

3. In the **Application** menu, click the Office for Mac app (**Microsoft Excel**, **Microsoft Word**, **Microsoft PowerPoint**, **Microsoft OneNote**, **Microsoft Outlook**) you want to create keyboard a shortcut for.
4. Enter a **Menu Title** and the **Keyboard Shortcut** and click **Add**.

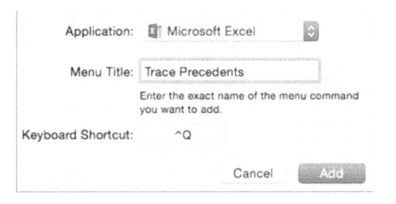

Tip: If you aren't sure what the menu name is for a command, click **Help** in that app and search for what you want, which will then show you the exact menu name.

CHAPTER 6.

Keyboard Shortcuts In OneNote 2016 for Mac.

Definition of Program: Microsoft OneNote 2016 for Mac is a program designed by Microsoft Corporation for effective note-taking by Macintosh computer users.

Frequently Used Shortcuts

The following table shows the most frequently used shortcuts in OneNote 2016 for Mac.

TASK	SHORTCUT
Select all items on the current page.	⌘+ A (Continue pressing to expand the scope of your selection.)
Select the page title.	⌘+ Shift + T
Cut the selected text or item.	⌘+ X
Copy the selected text or item to the clipboard.	⌘+ C
Paste the contents of the clipboard.	⌘+ V
Undo the last action.	⌘+ Z

Redo the last action.	⌘+ Y
Open notebook.	Shift+⌘ + O
Close notebook.	⌘+ W
Indent a paragraph from the left of a word.	Tab
Indent a paragraph from anywhere in a paragraph.	⌘+ Closing bracket ( ])
Remove a paragraph indent from the left.	Shift + Tab or ⌘+ Opening bracket ([ )
Zoom in	Shift + Tab or ⌘+ Plus sign (+)
Zoom out	Shift + Tab or ⌘+ Minus sign (-)
Reset zoom	⌘+ Zero (0)
Collapse an expanded outline.	Control + Shift + Plus sign (+)
Expand a collapsed outline.	Control + Shift + Minus sign (-)
Open a link.	Select link + Return
Copy the format of the selected text.	Option + ⌘+ C
Paste the copied text format to selected text.	Option + ⌘+ V
Start dictation	Fn + Fn
Insert emodi	Control + ⌘+ Space

Get Started

If a function key doesn't work as you expect it to, press the Fn key in addition to the function key. If you don't want to press the Fn key every time, you can change your Apple system preferences.

Change function key preferences with the mouse

1. On the **Apple** menu, press **System Preferences**.
2. Select **Keyboard**.
3. On the **Keyboard** tab, select the check box for **Use all F1, F2, etc** as standard function keys.

Change function key preferences with the keyboard

1. Press ⌘+ Spacebar. You hear "Spotlight System dialog," and you're instructed to type. Type sys and press Enter.
2. You hear "System Preferences." The focus is in the search window.
3. Type **a** and then press the Down arrow key until you hear "Accessibility, completion selected." Press Enter. The **Accessibility** dialog opens, allowing you to set preferences.
4. Press the Tab key until you hear "You are currently in a table."
5. Press the Down arrow key until you hear "Keyboard." Press the Tab key to move to the **Open Keyboard Preferences** button and press the Spacebar.
6. Press the Tab key until you hear "Use all F1, F2, etc. as standard function keys." The focus is on a

1

check box. To select the check box, press the
Spacebar.

7. To save your changes and close the dialog box,
press ⌘+ Option + W.

Shortcut conflicts

Some Windows keyboard shortcuts conflict with the
corresponding default Mac OS keyboard shortcuts.
This topic flags such shortcuts with an asterisk. To use
these shortcuts, you may have to change your Mac
keyboard settings to change the Show Desktop shortcut
for the key.

Change system preferences for keyboard shortcuts with the mouse

1. On the **Apple** menu, press **System Preferences**.

   Note: To use System Preferences, you must have
   full keyboard access turned on.

2. Press **Keyboard**
3. Press the **Shortcuts** tab.
4. Click **Mission Control**.
5. Clear the check box for the keyboard shortcut
   that you want to use.

If you need to perform this function with the keyboard,
only please see the topic

Insert Content

TASK	SHORTCUT
Insert a line break without starting a new paragraph.	Shift + Return
Insert a line break.	Shift + Return
Insert the current date.	⌘+ D
Insert the current date and time.	⌘+ Shift + D
Insert equations (or convert selected text to a math equation).	Control + Equal sign (=)
Use Smart Lookup	Control + Option + ⌘+ L

Delete Content

TASK	SHORTCUT
Delete character to the left of cursor.	Delete
Delete character to the right of the cursor.	fn + Delete
Delete one word to the left.	Option + Delete
Delete one word to the right.	fn + Option +Delete or Option + Del

Move The Cursor

TASK	SHORTCUT
Move one character to the left.	Left Arrow

Move one character to the right.	Right Arrow
Move one word to the left.	Option +Left Arrow
Move up a line.	Up Arrow
Move down a line.	Down Arrow
Move to the beginning of the line.	⌘+ Left Arrow
Move to the end of the line.	⌘+ Right Arrow
Move to the beginning of the word to the left.	Option + Left Arrow
Move to the ending of the word to the right.	Option + Right Arrow
Go to next paragraph.	⌘+ Up Arrow
Go to previous paragraph.	⌘+ Down Arrow
Scroll up in the current page.	Page Up
Scroll down in the current page.	Page Down
Go to the top of the page.	Command + Up Arrow
Go to the bottom of the page.	Command + Down Arrow
Go to the next paragraph.	Option + Up Arrow
Go to the previous paragraph.	Option + Down Arrow

Format Tables

TASK	SHORTCUT
Create a table.	Tab

Create another column in a table with a single row.	Tab
Create another row when at the end cell of a table. NOTE: Press Return a second time to finish the table.	Return
Create a column to the right of the current column in a table.	⌘+ Option+ R
Create a column to the left of the current column in a table.	⌘+ Option + ECommand+Option+E didn't work for me.
Create a row below the current row in a table.	⌘+ Return
Create another paragraph in the same cell in a table.	Option + Return

Search

TASK	SHORTCUT
Search on the page.	⌘+ F
Search all notebooks.	⌘+ Option + F

Navigate Within a Notebook

TASK	SHORTCUT
Switch between sections in a notebook.	Option + Tab
Switch between pages in a section.	1. Start with the cursor within a page, then press Control + Tab. The focus moves to **Add Page**. 2. Press the Tab key to move the focus to your page. 3. Press the Up arrow key or Down arrow key to select the previous or next page in your section.
Move the selected paragraphs up.	⌘+ Shift + Up Arrow
Move the selected paragraphs down.	⌘+ Shift + Down Arrow
Move the selected paragraphs left (decreasing the indent).	⌘+ Shift + Left Arrow

Advanced Cursor Navigation

TASK	SHORTCUT

Move the insertion point up in the current page, or expand the page up.	⌘+ Option + Up Arrow
Move the insertion point down in the current page, or expand the page down.	⌘+ Option + Down Arrow
Move the insertion point left in the current page, or expand the page to the left.	⌘+ Option + Left Arrow
Move the insertion point right in the current page, or expand the page to the right.	⌘+ Option + Right Arrow

Other Commands

TASK	SHORTCUT
Open other notebooks or create new ones.	⌘+ O
View the list of your open notebooks.	Control + G
Create a new notebook page.	⌘+ N
Open the OneNote preferences.	⌘+ , (Comma)
Move page to another location.	⌘+ Shift + M
Copy page to another location.	⌘+ Shift + C
Move or copy page again to last selected section.	Option + ⌘+ T
Enter full-screen mode.	Control + ⌘ +_F
Synchronize this notebook.	⌘+ S
Synchronize all notebooks	Shift + ⌘+ S

CHAPTER 7.

The Bonus Section

Safari 9 (El Capitan): Safari Keyboard and Other Shortcuts.

Safari is an internet browser developed by Apple Inc. that goes with Mac computers. It is fast and more energy efficient than any other browser as far as browsing with Macintosh computers are concerned.

This is a list of keyboard shortcuts you can use, in addition to those that appear in Safari menus.

Webpages

TASK	SHORTCUT
Scroll up, down, left, or right	Press the arrow keys.
Scroll in larger increments	Press Option while you press an arrow key.
Scroll down a screen	Page Down Space bar
Scroll up a screen	Page Up Shift–Space bar

Scroll to the top-left or bottom-left corner of the page	Command–Up Arrow or Home Command–Down Arrow or End
Highlight the next item on a webpage	Tab highlights the next text field or pop-up menu. Tab also highlights buttons and other controls if "All controls" is selected in the Shortcuts pane of the Keyboard pane of System Preferences. Option-Tab highlights the same items as Tab plus all other clickable items. To swap the behavior of Tab and Option-Tab, turn on "Press Tab to highlight each item on a webpage" in the Advanced pane of Safari preferences.
Open a page in a new tab	Command-click a link Command-click a bookmark Command-Return after typing in the Smart Search field.
Open a page in a new tab, and bring the tab to the front	Shift-Command-click a link Shift-Command-click a bookmark

	Shift-Command-Return after typing in the Smart Search field.
Bring the next tab to the front	Control-Tab or Shift-Command-]
Bring the previous tab to the front	Control-Shift-Tab or Shift-Command -[
Select one of your first nine tabs	Command-1 to Command-9
Close all tabs except for one	Option-click the close button (X) on the tab you want to leave open
Open in tabs all the bookmarks in a folder in the Favorites bar	Command-click the folder in the Favorites bar
See a list of recent pages by name	Hold down the Back or Forward button until the list appears
See a list of recent pages by web address (URL)	Press Option and hold down the Back or Forward button until the list appears
Go to your homepage	Command-Home key
While typing in the Smart Search field, restore the current webpage address	Esc
Close Reader	Esc
Exit full-screen view	Esc

Download a linked file	Option-click a link to the file
Open a downloaded file	Double-click the file in the downloads list

Reading List

TASK	SHORTCUT
Add the current page	Shift-Command-D
Add a linked page	Shift-click a link to the page
Remove a page	Swipe left over the page summary using a trackpad or mouse that supports gestures, then click Remove. Or, swipe all the way to the left until the page summary disappears.

Bookmarks

TASK	SHORTCUT
Add a bookmark to the Favorites bar	Click the Smart Search field to show the page's full address and its icon, then drag the icon to the Favorites bar
Move a bookmark on the Favorites bar	Drag the bookmark left or right

Remove a bookmark from the Favorites bar	Drag the bookmark off the top of the bar

Bookmarks Sidebar and Bookmarks View

TASK	SHORTCUT
Select bookmarks and folders in the sidebar	Command-click each bookmark and folder Shift-click to extend the selection
Select the next bookmark or folder	Up Arrow or Down Arrow
Open the selected bookmark	Space bar
Open the selected folder	Space bar or Right Arrow
Close the selected folder	Space bar or Left Arrow
Open the selected folder and its subfolders in the sidebar	Option–Right Arrow
Close the selected folder and its subfolders in the sidebar	Option–Left Arrow
Change the name or address of a bookmark	Select the bookmark, then press Return
Cancel editing a bookmark name in the sidebar	Esc

Finish editing a bookmark name	Return
Create a folder containing the selected bookmarks and folders in bookmarks view	Option-click the New Folder button at the bottom of the window
Delete a bookmark	Select the bookmark, then press Delete

Customer's Page.

This page is for customers who enjoyed Microsoft OneNote 2016 Keyboard Shortcuts For Macintosh.

Dearly beloved customer, please leave a review behind if you enjoyed this book or found it helpful. It will be highly appreciated, thank you.

Download Our Free EBooks Today.

In order to appreciate our customers, we have made some of our titles available at 0.00. Totally free. Feel free to get a copy of the free titles.

(A) For Keyboard Shortcuts In Windows

Go to Amazon: Windows 7 Keyboard shortcuts

Go to Other Stores: Windows 7 Keyboard Shortcuts

(B) For Keyboard Shortcuts In Office 2016

Go to Amazon: Word 2016 Keyboard Shortcuts For windows

Go to Other Stores: Word 2016 Keyboard Shortcuts For Windows

Note: Feel free to download them from your favorite store today. Thank you!

Other Books By This Publisher.

S/N	Title	Series
Series A: Limits Breaking Quotes.		
1	Discover Your Key Christian Quotes	Limits Breaking Quotes
Series B: Shortcut Matters.		
1	Windows 7 Shortcuts	Shortcut Matters
2	Windows 7 Shortcuts & Tips	Shortcut Matters
3	Windows 8.1 Shortcuts	Shortcut Matters
4	Windows 10 Shortcut Keys	Shortcut Matters
5	Microsoft Office 2007 Keyboard Shortcuts For Windows.	Shortcut Matters
6	Microsoft Office 2010 Shortcuts For Windows.	Shortcut Matters
7	Microsoft Office 2013 Shortcuts For Windows.	Shortcut Matters
8	Microsoft Office 2016 Shortcuts For Windows.	Shortcut Matters
Series C: Teach Yourself.		
1	Teach Yourself Computer Fundamentals	Teach Yourself
Series D: For Painless Publishing		
1	Self-Publish it with CreateSpace.	For Painless Publishing
2	Where is my money? Now solved for Kindle and CreateSpace	For Painless Publishing
3	Describe it on Amazon	For Painless Publishing
4	How To Market That Book.	For Painless Publishing